The Open Hand of Sky

poems by

Connie Wasem Scott

Finishing Line Press
Georgetown, Kentucky

The Open Hand of Sky

Publisher: Leah Huete de Maines

Editor: Christen Kincaid

Cover Art: *Shine Through The Spaces* by Shelli Walters,
    ShelliWaltersStudio.com

Author Photo: Makenna Haeder, photographer

Cover Design: Elizabeth Maines McCleavy

Order online: www.finishinglinepress.com
    also available on amazon.com

Author inquiries and mail orders:
Finishing Line Press
P. O. Box 1626
Georgetown, Kentucky 40324
U. S. A.

Table of Contents

3 :: trees

for Makenna

I know there is still time—
time for the hands
to open, for the bones of them
to be filled
by those failed harvests of want….

~ Galway Kinnell
"Still Time"

1 :: fire

The wind moves through the highest tree branches
without seeming to hurt them.

Tell me.
Who was I when I used to call your name?

> ~ Marie Howe
>   "Prayer"

The Punch Line

My mother tells me a joke involving
two Swedes and a russet potato. She no longer
lives in the house where the purple irises
searched for the sun each evening when it fell
like a toppled streetlight behind the house.
My mother's hands grew like branches
of birch trees, or their roots, long
and sinewy and reaching for the ivory
keys of the old upright in the basement. The joke
really isn't funny. What's funny
is I can't remember the punch line.
Come here once, my mother's mother
often said. *Bist du krank?* We were children
back then, my brother and I, whacking
each other with rhubarb stalks
in the sunny yard, rhubarb Mom grew
for jam and that sauce Dad liked
over ice cream. I'm the one in a jam now.
My brother's hands have disappeared.
This too shall pass, Mom often said.
She wasn't joking. I fold her
hankie into an envelope. She doesn't want to
set me down. I cling to the pink blanket
she's draped over my head as she carries me
across the street while it snows.

Chemistry

Hydrogen is the most abundant element.
It makes up 75% of all mass. Yet the atom
has only two parts—
one electron orbits one proton.
This tiny atom also saturates the dark heavens
with light—hydrogen clusters burst
supernova blue and magenta against the galaxy's
black skies.
        My brother got his first chemistry set
in fifth grade. I watched him tinker with test tubes
and transform two clear solutions into liquid garnets,
the same color as the petunias Mom's best friend
grew all over her back yard. My brother
controlled the elements—water that passed
through his hands became jewels.
He set up slides of pond water
on his microscope to show me the world
teems with life we can't see
with our eyes.
        In 1766, Henry Cavendish
observed hydrogen made water when it
burned. Who knew a certain kind of fire
can put itself out? In 1806, Humphry Davy
discovered the *"true nature of bonding"*
is that a bond can be broken in half.
Hydrogen is the lightest element,
but it contains enough power
to lift people clear into the sky.

The Whiskers on His Face

Grandpa Frank loved onions and mustard.
I can still smell his breath, feel
the whiskers he scraped
against my brother's face and mine.
I loved the scraping, his breath,
his game of clamping his arms round our necks
till we laughed, stuck in his lap.
That's all I remember of him.

My mother gave me his sweater
after he died. It was amber like wheat,
the wool rough as his whiskers.
I wore it a year. Yellow buttons
the color of his breath, his bones
the size of mine at thirteen. I could trace
the sea in the seams, follow the listing ship
that carried him across the Atlantic at two.
The sweater gave me his passage,
the reason his bones remained
small as the handbag he slept in
those months beyond land.

The sweater grew a hole in the elbow.
I gave it up. My aunts tell me
the ship sank in the harbor.
I want to sink to my grandpa in his grave,
to his dust, what's left of his bones,
the odor of tubers stained on his teeth.
He freezes each winter in the North Dakota plains,
but when the soil warms in May,
he grows restless, his fingers
wiggle like worms: *it's time to make hay.*

Trees, Paper, Time, Hands

I want to remember the two white birch trees my dad planted
in our front yard, how they started off skinny as my six-year-old arms,
then grew thick as my winter-white legs. By then, the bark began
to behave like birch bark behaves—the trunk released curled sheets
of its skin. The tree's own skin was sheets of white paper. I
drew on them with fingertip and thumb. One night, the bark
looked like my grandmother's white hair, and when the ground
was covered with snow and all the bushes white
and the trees white without leaf, the branches grew
into my mother's outstretched hands.

Daily Bread

Their sandals flap like beating wings.
The girl shoulders her mother's hand
along the pond where ducks and geese
climb onto the grass, their long necks stretched
for a piece of torn bread the boy offers
by hand. He peers into the eyes
of a swan. The children thrill
for the birds' waxy bills close at hand,
how they tug the bread, hunger
blowing away their fear. A thunderstorm

grumbles in the mountains
to the west. The boy listens
for the rain, knows that seasons come
and go, this lake will freeze, will hold
these breadcrumbs and leaves until spring.
The girl lives closer to feathers.
She knows her mother
smells like moss and wet trees,
her father fills the lake with rings,
her brother's smile
is a rippled pond and she
rests there, a tuft
of white down.

Mom's Biceps

I'm standing beside her as she brushes her hair.
Her arm swells with each stroke. A cedar
box of hair pins rests next to her white bottle
of Jergens. The fleshy hills in her arms
embarrass her. She tells me they grew
hard from milking cows each dawn
and dusk with her sisters.
They're not ladylike, she says,
or something close to it. I think
my mother's blood is fresh cream.

We drive in our black Comet to a farm
south of town where Mrs. Lindt greets us
wiping her hands on an apron, says she
knows our car from half mile away. We
follow her into the kitchen where the morning
cream cools in a crock, watch her ladle
ivory ribbons into the gaping mouths
of Mason jars we brought from home.

Mom stands tall as the poplars
in the wind break that runs from the barn
to the house. She tells me she liked
separating cream the best, how it
speckled her clothing and skin.
I want to dip my tongue in a bowl
like a barn cat while she talks.

Slaughterhouse

My best friend's dad worked in the slaughterhouse
at Monfort's whose feedlots spread like prairie grass
north of town. I never knew for sure, but
I imagined Mr. Nickels was the man who
put the cows down, poised at the chute's dead end
raising a lead mallet, the wood handle

worn pale from his hand. I believed he tried
not to look in the animals' fist-sized eyes before he
hammered the white stars on their heads
then carted their carcasses to the man who opened
their throats with a blade. Blood spilled from their necks
like red shawls, blood so thick the men
needed boots, and rows of dead cows filing by on hooks
pulled by cables that squealed. The butchers' frocks

were stained like red finger paintings
smeared by kids. The feedlots often
muddied the air. That's when I wondered how
Mr. Nickels could drive to that smell every day,
don his rubber boots and walk the cement floors
to his place where Clorox barely masked
the stench of blood and ripped hides.
In the lockers after his shift, he scrubbed his hands
until they turned red. On his way home each night

he stopped for a six pack of Schlitz and some Kents.
At home he filled a kitchen seat and smiled
at Chris and me with bloodshot eyes, his raven hair
shiny and combed. I suppose he tried to erase
the mistake of meat with those beers. That's what
he did most nights if he wasn't driving a truck load
of girls to Campus Delight for dilly bars and cones.

Years after we moved, they gave him a pink slip.
Now he's the janitor at our old school. I imagine he
sweeps the halls, sponges the blue and white

ceramic tiles, and hums while he wipes the sinks
splattered with pink-powdered soap and droplets of red
and blue and green from the first graders' water-based paints.

Night's Coming

A brother and a sister play like wildings in a field.
Night's coming to darken the clouds and
their whispers that breathe along the cottonwoods
lining long gullies of shadows and swollen cattails.

Night's come to darken the clouds and
the sister who fingers the breeze while her long hair
lines a gully of shadows and swollen cattails.
Her brother soothes her scraped knee with cool mud.

The sister fingers the breeze with her long hair
growing like branches of trees. The wind whistles.
Her brother soothes her knee with cool mud
but she cries. They grow frightened and run

from growing branches of trees. The wind whistles
their whispers along the breathing cottonwoods
and she cries. They've grown frightened and run,
this brother and sister who play wildly in the field.

Dream # 3: Spilled Milk

The fence post cracks in half from the top
to the base, so I step through it, make
my way past the compost bin where
I hear the amber syrup
ooze into earth. The daylight ties
my smile to a cloud that's smudged
with sunlight and shadow. The barn
blinks in the light where I peek
through a cracked door to see
big-eyed dairy cows spilling
their milk into pails. And there's
my brother, crying as he tugs
the pink teats. The breeze
blows in, wipes his face. We hold
our hands and head home.

We Watched for Falling Stars

Summer skies brought us together—three cousins
driving out of a North Dakota town until the right dirt road
crested some farmer's hill. We parked in the center
of the road, stepped out under a sky so black we'd almost
gasp at the reckoning, a third eye deeper than water.
The green broth of alfalfa, sweet clover, and mustard—
aromas that awakened our brains while I lay on the hood
of Rod's car, Charlie a horse length away at the edge
of a field. Springsteen wailed from the stereo
like a prophet: *it ain't no sin to be glad you're alive.*
We could never see enough of that sky. The truth

for us those nights we watched for shooting stars
was everything bright and shiny streaking past our eyes.
Truth was the space between our words that grew
long tails of silence as we gaped at the sky.
A cool breeze blew back our hair. In the cities
that grew far from there, the Milky Way fell like asphalt
into the lighted sea of streetlamps and headlights.

But on that prairie, the stars were brighter than our lives.
It wouldn't have mattered then to know
one of us would shoot away one day
like the stars falling above, burning into a long ray
of light that sparks and dies. We wouldn't have believed it.
We lit cigarettes, tapped the smoke out our mouths
in rows of Os, rising like incense to the sky.

He Carried My Voice

Part 1

Lisa said it started at dinner: he fell straight back in his chair,
his eyes rolled up white. *Opportunistic. Meningitis.* The words
infected our mouths. I chewed them into his hospital room
where I stroked his face, my brother, whose words
crackled off his tongue like tangled wires. His body settled
in bed for this sister breath soothing the nest of his mouth.
By dawn, the light left his eyes.
                              He'd gotten away, my young man
who once fished with our father in the mountains for trout,
who shared with me secrets of pond grass, the currents of ice
slipstreaming rocks, and branches that shadow dark fins
toward the light. I brought him ice to stiffen his loose tongue.
Something bubbling inside his skull was breaking his scalp
into scales, his mind like fishing line caught on a branch.

Part 2

I did not leave him, like a photo at bedside.
One day I lifted him from the crumpled bed
to the vinyl chair by the window. His body had grown
old, his eyes clouded into tiny cups of milk.
Usually, the nurse changed his diaper.
That day the job was mine to clean the mess
between his legs and wipe the place where
chemo in his urine burned his skin.
A brother's penis felt out of place in my hand,
like I was handling someone's eyeball or tongue.
The morning light slanted toward his face with little trace
of sun, his body limp as wet laundry.
                              So I made him
lift his arms one by one, stretch his hands and tired legs
like a puppet blown by a fan. I wanted to save his life,

not make him wet his hospital pants. The trickle sounded
the tile beneath his chair and swamped the room with a sour
stench like vinegar and eggs that stopped his wife and son
at the door. They found him sleeping in the chair, his head
lobbed to the side, his mouth parted with some drool, me
on my hands and knees with a towel.

Part 3

Today I found this photo in a drawer—my nephew's arm
wraps my brother's neck like a scarf, his teeth more white
against a face burned red by radiation to his head.
A new corduroy cap dresses his bald scalp. In a blink
of days, the outer layer of his brain will be erased
when it rises like dough against the skull of his pain.
An angel dresses the Christmas tree above him
like a nurse. His son pouts for the camera, his
lower lip large and red like a bruise.
                                    Reeling
in a smaller place for children, my brother
carried my voice like a lunch box. His hurried words
rushed out in pairs of skinned knees. We waved
bye-bye like he was still five and me three. He'll be
taught the facts of his life again like crumbs.
                                    I framed him
in silver on my desk. His arms fold across his chest
like a promise, his face as patient as a boy teaching a sister
how to count. The face on his watch a blank glare.

Sleepwalking

You fell into a darker sleep
with no stars to guide you. Dawn
fills the gaps between the mountains
without you. Without you, the blue sky
fades to pale hay. Every valley
we ever walked through forgets
the sound of your name.

I wonder the paths your
mind takes, why you walk
in circles like the words
you repeat, as if saying them
again and again will straighten
them out, as if dropped
like crumbs they'll lead you home.

To Protect Your Brother's Young Sons

Rip your sunglasses off your face and fling them
out the speeding car window. Let them be
pulverized a hundred times an hour for being useless.

Collect a thumb-sized bottle of pool water where he
taught his first son to dive off his shoulders headfirst.
Sprinkle a few drops on the boys' frosted flakes.

His name draws shadows across his sons' faces like drapes.
Give the boys cloven leaves of creosote that smell like rain.
Bring sunlight and rough muffins to dunk in their milk.

Keep your blue hospital scrubs. Stuff the legs with bags
of all the hope you hoarded. Stitch them into two
teddy bears. Draw a smile on each one.

Dream # 7: Dark Angels

I dream I'm drowning
in a flood. Doused
streets bob and pitch.
Portions of asphalt
break off. The pounding

disturbs me. Surely
I will kick and sink and wake up
at the foot of some stairs.
At birth, I failed,
my water sac drying.

The hushed steps of wet cats
whisk away the shadows
and harps of dark angels.
There will be more sunlight soon.

I forget all the hallways
and rooms I must locate.
A fast, thin slip
of water lets me go
dangerous as a sinner
in the first offense.

Aubade, with Open Hand

Morning is a face you must recall
    because you lost your brother
        overnight. This must be him, sitting
            on a park bench at 5 a.m., rustling

through lists that collect in his pouch
    like seeds. Your mother calls you to say
        he rose before dawn, let himself
            out of the house and walked

three miles of city streets to find
    his wife and sons. He made his way
        to their house, even though
            he can't sustain a thought longer

than lightning. For a minute this morning,
    you thought you heard him call your name.
        His voice came to you on a breeze
            like a hand with soft fingers, palm opened.

To Bring Back His Memory

Lift your muscle-weary hope off the pavement.
Stuff it into the buckskin pouch that held
flintstones you collected near your grandmother's house.

While Orion strikes his pose above the hospital,
pray he guards this man who *never needed
anybody's help in any way.*

When it comes, bring the ocean inside you (even
inside your car, the undulant inner tide rocking).

Lift your fist above a bowl of Russian thistle you
stole from the forest. Sing to the heavens. Believe
he'll hear your voice and follow you home.

Dream # 11: Peeping Tom

The delivery boy arrives
wearing a different
color than the one
we expect.
Terri forgets
how the song goes.
So we go for a drive
with the stereo turned up
too loud. John
makes a wrong turn. We're
lost for months.

We drop to our knees
at our front door.
The red paint
pales before our eyes. I
can't reach the doorbell.
Inside, we hear the music
died. Tomorrow
appears like a stranger
peeking through the drapes.

It Never Came Back

When dandelions spread their jagged leaves
beneath the elms in our yard and the grass
in the field across the street grew hip high,
you'd call me out of the house and we'd race
to the field that swallowed us whole into grass
that tickled our legs with small grain heads.
One day we ran to the cottonwood grove
where you pointed to an empty blue eggshell
at our feet, smaller than eyes, small as our
thumbnails combined. You showed me
a patch of moss shaped like a horse head
near the pond where tadpoles ricocheted like gnats.
And before the day hungered its way to a stove,
the wind whipped us out of the trees at full run,
and we wondered where the boomerang you threw once
touched down. We watched that red plastic V
sail across the field like hope before slicing thick grass.
It never came back. Today I search the ponds
of your eyes stilled by illness for some glimpse
of that sky, a patch of moss, an empty shell
rocking our hands—any flash of memory
winging like a broken bird through the air.

Under the Beds

for the clients at Tangram Rehab for brain-injured adults
San Marcos, TX

Sam's baritone voice softens us the way
magnolia blooms ease the day with their shade.
He bounced his life off the dash of his car to live
here at Tangram where the blue marker charts his progress
on the white-board down the hall. Sam helps the others
sweep the walks, tuck clean sheets on their beds, carry
their plates to the sink after meals.

Brian's river is dammed up
for good. His right arm
knotted to driftwood.
Water pools behind his eyes.
A clump of words escapes
his mouth like a trout. His smile
is sunlight bouncing
for a second off a wave.

Charlie works at the bookstore
in town where he helps the worn
paperbacks find their places
on shelves. Some days, he copies titles
on the faint lines of index cards.
He's forgotten the words
that would fill the blanks of his life.

Cory's ATV dented his head. His left eye
moved away from his face. His past he says
is like looking into the sea
near his home in Alaska—ice
clouds the clear waters beneath.
At seventeen, he's the youngest.
Cory wants to kiss me.
He holds a bit of my heart in his teeth.

Sorrow is a Jagged Bone

The sorrows we collect each day slip
into our joints while we dream.
One woman's stiff shoulder
is the mother who died before the red canna
bloomed in the yard. Another's inflamed wrist
is the brother found floating in the canal,
bloated like an overstuffed flour sack.
Tears that never escape weaken
the spines of our muscles. At the break

of day when we rise
predictable as fire, our pain returns
to scratch morning's smooth face.
The sorrow must be rebroken
like a poorly set bone.

After dinner, when we rest ourselves
like cats, our eyes grow small.
Something our bodies know
starts gathering the shards. Pain,
even splintered, makes its way
into the tunnels of our bones.

Nothing We Did Before

It is because he fought
to live he now lives
without history. For him,
the future died more fully than the past.
He became a child, unable
to die for anyone.
                    Listen, I didn't
lose anything—a song,
my name, a knee scar. My brother
lives on, unable to leave
footprints of memory.
He now has many opportunities
to be forgotten.
                    I've learned
to protect his loss. The moon didn't cause
the night to die. Sure, that was the end:
nothing we did before will matter
to anyone else.

Truth Is,

you won't know what to do, how to carry the bag
in your chest, the one filled with sand you need for
traction to get out of the jam you're in. Step one
is to scour the sky for a cloud that resembles
your brother's hand. Breathe deeply while you search,
and soon, your heart may quiet, not quiet the way
he lay lifeless when you last left him, but pond-water
quiet, crack-of-dawn quiet. Alive, just not making
a ruckus about it. At this point, with your best
I once sang in the church choir voice, break
a loud *focoso* free from your chest and
curse those damned gods in the heavens for paring him down
like a shriveled potato in the first place, *d.c. al coda*
the hell out of that song, repeating as often as you need,
to hell with the damnation you once feared might rain down
from above. You're not in a Sophocles play, so
belt it out like a lightning bolt. Take another deep breath,
then tether your gaze on the nearest tree (get creative if no
trees are around you—a fire escape or a smokestack will do), really
latch on with your gaze, the way a stubborn homeowner
who refuses to evacuate a hurricane clings for dear
life to a lamp post. Stay there like his body will stay
when he's scattered next to that fallen tree in the Rockies.
Let those clutched hands of your eyes trace the lines
of that tree from the base where it sits, to the tiniest
twig at the top. Rest there for a minute, think how
your perspective looking up is a world different
from the view looking down. That's
how it's going to be from now on.

After the Fire

Stand on the edge of the burnt forest.
You could count the number of black lines
of former trees, but why? They'll still
be dead despite those hopeful tufts of needles
clinging to the tops, as though each
charred pine wants to be a torch
that can be set on fire again. How many
times can one fire burn? How many times
can one man die? I knew a man who died
many times for years. Now we can see
past that and notice the mountain
through these black sticks that scratch
our view innumerable times.

2 :: sand

such a slip of minutes
as if someone got her wish

we could live in pink   holding a shining note
release   someone else's anger

> *~ Naomi Shihab Nye*
>   *"Each Day We Are Given So Many Gifts"*

Oology

I went to Franks's Hatchery when I was a kid, watched
the ladies candle eggs in front of bare light bulbs.
A spot like a mole meant the yolk took hold.
They set those shells beneath wide-eyed lamps
until the tiny beaks released the chicks—yellow
as the marigolds our neighbor raised in his yard. I gazed

at the blossoms through the chain link fence. The red
of some petals startled me like wounds. I liked
the multi-colored marigolds the best, a blend
of yolk and blood like the fertilized egg Mom cracked
into cake batter she was beating in a bowl. I haven't
dyed an Easter egg for years, but I remember the colors

turned out paler than we hoped. In college I dyed
Ukrainian eggs, dribbled wax then dipped the eggs
in colored baths until they dazzled like a box of new paints.
We didn't cook those eggs so their insides would dry up
and not rot. Last year, one of those colorful
hollow shells shattered in my hand.

My husband just bought a dozen jumbo eggs. When I broke
the four I fry for Sunday brunch, each egg revealed
its double yolk—four pairs of yellow eyes
gaped from the pan. They helped me search
for the germ of life as I held up our marriage
in front of the kitchen window's morning light.

They Leave Slim Holes

Outside our home a thistle field
withers in a lava bed that's settled
its hide under sand. We've grown
used to the lizards' monochrome skin
and dirt too poor to bank rain.
Our eyes and hands don't touch
as we walk single file, kind words
as scattered as these clumps
of clouds that litter the sky. We hike
stiff as knives. Sometimes

we lower ourselves
under fences far from home,
walk on smooth rocks bedding
a stream where grass
and cool mud ease our feet.
One month we mended
wounds from barbed wire, another
we smeared poultice on our legs
where fireweed left its red sting.

Yesterday we hiked again
in the desert, hoping we'd be
buoyed by wind. We took off our boots
when we got home and plucked
the goat-head stickers
piercing the soles. They leave
slim holes when they're picked.

Tarot Reading: Passion (inverted)

A man and woman stand under a tree.
Red fruit clings to the branches and their arms
rise naturally to pick it. They stand
nude beneath the tree holding their hands
with sweet fingers. Their feet have
rooted the soil, but the world has turned
upside down. They do not yet feel
the blood rush to their hands.

A shadow prowls near the tree
and watches the woman and man
to see how they'll act when the gravity
hits and makes them see,
finally, their uplifted hands turn
slowly red inside and out.

Tracking Orbs

You can see the rings with binoculars,
my friend said, pointing to Saturn,
it's so close. So I set up my telescope to see
the inky rings and red swirls for myself
before the planet moves on.

•

The twinge a woman feels
when an egg launches into her dark
tubes is called *mittelschmerz,* the 'middle pain'
of protest against the void,
the meddling ache that cries
give me life.

•

The calendar becomes my chart—each day
I track my basal temps, circle the numbers
for days of blood, X's for sex—a calculus
I use to pinpoint the launch.

•

The fear that made me
back down and say *leave me alone*
becomes a space to be filled.
The darkness grows
crowded with wanting.

•

Wrap a river
rock in blue cloth.
Place the bundle
near her empty
womb to draw out
the delay.

•

I can't fix Saturn in my sights.
I've lost that burning
orb in this star-crowded sky.
The telescope wobbles in my fumbling
hands which have grown
impatient as Mercury tonight.

study: alarm

I clock the time
it takes him to pinch
sleep off at the roots
and rise rumpled
from our bed. His limbs
stir slowly, fixed to the still
waters that run his dream
deep into the green
grass clumped at his feet.
We can't afford to waste
time—our bed is burning,
our house, our words,
all burning beyond the jet spray
of love that could save us.

Projections

Something's here
that's not been here before.
It feels like a water balloon,
or a bagged guppy. No,
it's a small cave where she
floats, my baby albino fish
who's starting to grow

eyes. I can picture her peering
into my water's deep sky, plush walls
dark all around her. She's
tethered by a water snake
that writhes. Does she think
about scrawling crude creatures
on the walls? Does she
dream of a flickering

fire and smell my dry skin?
Is she sucking her thumb
like the cigarette she'll light
after she first has sex with a
boy in a motel on the outskirts
of town? I feel her
flutter like a raucous song-
bird thrumming her cage.

Motion of Rocks

I woke early this morning to watch the craggy-faced mountain
shift colors with the rising light. I thought I heard singing
as I stood in the garden, my water breaking
before the sun. We followed the mountain's spine
that stretches south then tapers and dips underground
downtown near the hospital that receives me
with a bedrock for birthing. I feel the mountain's magnetic arms
through the polished linoleum. A brush of her fingers
turns the skin of my belly to stone.
I am a granite woman walking this lit tunnel
hefting a boulder past other caves where
great women moan and calve, that one
is calving right now, I hear her howl, then

I'm gripped by a seismic shift grinding
my insides into a hot boulder fissure
cracking open. How quickly we learn
the body of a woman contains magma.
My stone belly rocks in geo-elastic waves,
core shocked into shudders
that shudder, and the masked woman
cries *tilt your hips!* so I shift and erupt
my child into her hands,

and before my baby's breath
can blast beyond her rock-round
cheeks, before the lust for mother
milk spills into her mouth like a
riddle she must solve to live,
her mind is a tongue
of fire lashing out
of my substratum into life.

Nestling

Except for the open plains of daylight
after we begin to sleep and are held
captive and in good company,
except for the white bricks
of our small house all the neighbors can see,
we are alone, tugging each other,
while the day smooths over us like water
and tumbles away from the bed.

We forget the coolness of untouched skin,
we forget the songs the summer wind
thrums through the trees. Our retreat
stirs these layers of lavender sheets—
your pod-like feet tucked in the nook
of my bent hips, your small head
burrowing the plush of my breast.

Even the dogs can't disturb us,
for we have sealed our ears against
the afternoon. Our mouths forget
everything except our warm skin.
We're tight clams remembering
milky pearls made slowly of sand
no swimmer can reach.

From the Well

Her hands are yeasty balls
of dough, raised under a towel
in the kitchen's warm corner.

She sucks on her fist as though
milk will squirt from the knuckles.
Her life depends upon it.

The plains spill across
the continent like
ribs of pale sand.

Daughter, will you tap the water
our mothers hauled in pails
from the well behind the house?

She smiles and her toothless gums
gleam like wet stones in the house's
north shade after a prayed-for rain.

The Butterfly Above Her Crib

I dreamt I found her in a murky tub,
submerged, too still. Thank god she took my breath
and I woke up. Today a driver cut me off,
he'd lost control, I knew for sure we'd crash.
Death's quick like that. I shook the whole way
home where I tidied her clothes while she napped.
I got out my pastels and stepstool to draw
a butterfly above her crib, mixed rose
with teal and smeared them on the wall so if
I die she'll have these wings to fill her eyes
with me, at least for a spell. I'm scared she'll die
and I'll be left with empty arms, the vacant
crib a monster's soul-less eye. I fear the dark
coiled rope my heart would be, were she to go.

I Let Go My Grip

I wait heavily in
dark sheets beside you
for your advance: a palm
opened, a limb
nudged. I lie
still, wanting
not to startle
your feeble hand with a stir.
I count your slow breaths

and soon hover
in the same cool sheets
above this still pond
green leaves scatter.
Shadows
invite my weight
down, ripples
lure me deep
into green. I do
not touch you but let

go my grip
on this overhung birch
and slip
past the leaves
into sleep.

How to Measure a Marriage Bed

The blinds we drape before our eyes
       can be lifted like the white flags

of silence we raise each dawn. We might
       believe we'll one day wed our blood-

red thoughts to the blue words
       spilling from these pens we hold

like bevel squares, measuring what we have
       against what we want. The fires

blazing in your eyes and in mine will soon
       be fed by fierce wind.

I come to know thirst

can be stuffed in a bag and carried
        beyond the city's rock walls, beyond the desert
                arroyos sealed in cement and the alleys
                        where broken names and bottles
                                glisten like fresh paint.

My dogs sleep on the sandy cement porch,
        far from the streets that never stop
                grumbling, where asphalt covers the ancient
                        seabed that perished long ago and
                                buried its bones in the sand.

As far as I can see a raggy range
        of rocks butts the sky. Sunshine
                hardens the landscape and grows
                        like lichen on my skin. I see the desert's smaller
                                hands—tiny cloven leaves of the creosote bush,

a sand dune's puckered hide. People
        on both sides of the river dream
                of crossing her bed. The sky
                        takes up more room here. A bride on the edge
                                of town rips off her lipstick and cries.

Tarot Reading: The Hanged Man (inverted)

It's clear he'll never be happy. He's
        strung up by an ankle
                and hangs from a tree.

Shall I read into this?
        Project onto the tree
                the role of the father,

the hands that strung him up
        first? See how he tucks
                his hands behind his back.

What is he hiding? This card's
        inverted, it appears the man is
                standing on one leg, the other

crooked at the knee like he's
        relaxed, but he's never at ease, he's pulled
                down by forces he can't see. See

that band of yellow light that
        arcs around his head? Don't be fooled.
                That's no golden halo of a saint.

The Day Your Dad Died

for PK

The phone rings and the news
swells and pitches like a sleeper
tossing on his thin mattress
of goodbyes. Your father

lay down, jabbed his pale finger
into the belly of air, which for him
disappeared into the ER's bright
lamp on the ceiling. You should have

never seen his face that an orderly
pulled from a drawer, his head
propped on a brick, eyelids drooped
above his reaped eyes. Listen

to him sway away from the sky
overhead, trying one last time
to kick through the brambles
between you. The room left

his face like a whisker
or an ache. He was always
receding. You did not see
his meek wave stir the air.

Harvest

Lama Mountain
Taos, New Mexico

Bonnie brought the clay jar to our table
where it rested all week in the clutter
of our poems. The potter
used a brush thick as a rosebud
to paint green vines along the jar's lip
and a woman who reaches for red
berries in the vines with hands that appear
strong enough to pull sucker trees
from fields.

•

Who watches the children
when the women have all gone
to pick berries? The women lose
themselves in the bush, rest
against the mossy skin of cool rocks.
Scarves sleeve their forearms
against brambles. They return with dark
stains on their fingers and tongues.

•

When my mother brings me dill
from her garden, the flower heads
heavy with pollen more yellow than
butterfly weed dried in the sun, the aroma
lingers like the songs of black crickets
at nightfall. Pollen clings
to the arms of her blouse.

Steps To Protect Your Young Child

1: Take the ring-necked pheasant feather your aunt mailed you,
   a blue columbine you grew from a seed,
   a sprig of creosote from the desert near your house.
   Grind them into a poultice to heal her.

2: Warm seven smooth stones in your hands.
   Picture your desert daughter selecting them from a shallow lake.
   Arrange the stones in a circle, set her inside until
   they flare into torches around her.

3: Let go of all those salty drops, those
   tiny silver scales. Collect them.
   Sprinkle on the crown of her head.

study: dawn is a pool of blood

Before the blue tapestry of dawn unfurls along sky's
right hip, a red bolt of night slits her flesh and makes her

bleed where the air and dust mingle, rending the birth
of day quietly crimson with a violet whimper

only small creatures can hear. Dark waters, hold
still your awakening before you dash down the throats

of grassblades, up the ankles of berrystalks. Slip into slim
shadows the stars left along roadsides to warn us and

under the pale hides of quaking trees. Red, the raspy song
of life, of death. Red, the first pigment of dawn.

The Shape of My Hand

We sat together in the yard
gazing at October's last show of green
leaves and grass when the new moon
slipped behind some clouds,
washing all the greens a dull gray,
gray as the cement under our picnic bench.
I saw a handful of crickets dried in a web there.
Some say the new moon makes men more kind.
But that night, I doubted your kindness,
having watched it come and go as quick
as desert rain. So I let go of your hand.

Let's get out of the desert, you said.
I wanted to stay. For a moment,
we relaxed in our wanting,
our shadows beside us, locked in the sand.
Then the slim moon returned and faced us
with the back of her head.
That's why we left: no rain,
the moon's silence, the shape
of no one's obedient hand.

Tarot Reading: The Tower

The yellow tower squats atop
        a steep mountain. Lightning
                strikes the building into blaze, it's

toppling, the walls growing massive
        cracks. Flames shoot like angry
                canons out the one window

where a woman and man have leaped from
        and are falling, their limbs twisted
                and thrust out before them

as if their spindly arms could break
        their fall. The woman's face
                inside her flailing blue hair

looks calm, while tongues of flames
        lap the man's red shirt that billows
                behind him like superman's cape.

To Help My Young Daughter Move On

It's okay to cry. Gently
push the tears into the chambers of your face.
Feel your lungs grow pale like gills.
Inhale your tears.

Close your moss-green eyes, picture the sculptures you made
of sand-stuffed socks poking up from your sandbox
like a pod of sea serpents.
A sand-filled sock is your talisman.

Forget what I taught you about kindness.
Pour gasoline on the stuffed animals he gave you.
Torch them.
I'll help.

Let his coal-fire words blaze into flames with your toys
and smolder to ash. Shove the ashes
down the throat of your sand-sock
and tie it closed with a taut leather thread.

What Chance Did He Have

He didn't know I was made of clouds—
a body of air and water even
saints can't hold on to. Naturally,
eventually I dissipated, and my lacy
net of fog disappeared. What did he

know—he had leaped into my mist
half sheep, half hungry wolf
who'd lost most his fur.
It's like he hurried to me
because I wasn't afraid of his fear.

The same with the faded hammerhead
tattooed on his forearm,
and the washed-out mako on the other, each
unafraid and a hand's length away
from his touch. The sharks didn't help

his chances because this is what
sadness is, dry and unyielding, closed off
and drained of color. What chance did he
have when I remembered
the icy-fingered thrill of alone?

Vault

It's not because I grew tired
of sand, tired of its gritty
prayer for water, or of growing
tan by the sun and camouflaged
into the unending rocks. It was the
other desert I had to get out of, so
I packed my child and our toughened
skin into blue pullovers and blue jeans
and vaulted us out of that desert

where we discovered ourselves
preening in a mirror of river
pooled beside this grassy bank, stunned
by so much water—this fast-moving,
wild iris-lined stream. We kicked off
our shoes, squished the muddy
banks between our toes. I fondled
the small sticks she collected
and offered to me. They rattled
like dice in my hands.

3 :: trees

How it's easier

if we become more like a body of air, branches, and make room for this red charging thing that barrels through us.

~ Ada Limon
"Sway"

Into the Forest I Go

with thanks to John Muir

The park across the street's a small forest
I absorb through thirsty eyes and skin.
My deaf dog soaks it all in through his nose.
I go there when I'm losing my mind. Once I dropped it
on a muddy spring path. The ponderosas
guarded it till I found it and stuffed it
back into my head. Those massive pines

are the same age as the 111-year-old matriarch
we lost in windstorm. The treetop
stroked the face of our neighbor's
kitchen window when it fell. A logger
cut the trunk like a candy bar
divvied up by a mom with several kids.
I bet the uprooted root ball will remain a mass
of tangled arms in our yard for years,

but I'm no gambling man. I'm no man at all.
I was born when purple iris bloomed
in our flatland gardens near the Rockies.
The mountain I saw from my bedroom window
is a friend I've kept in touch with all these years.
Sometimes I see her grinning face

rimmed in a fur-lined parka.
She wears goose down all year. I would too if I lived
above the tree line, only small shrubs in every direction,
no limbs reaching for me no matter how long
I stand on the mountainside
with my face to the sun.

I Wish This Tree Were My Friend Jody

I look out the window at the red oak
by the curb, silhouetted in the sunlight
like a tall dancer on the sidewalk. Small fans
of spring leaves wave from each branch like a hankie.

I wish that tree were my friend Jody
carrying some treasure down the sidewalk
to show me—a silver charm, red pebble,
old photo of us, young. I'd run out the door
as she lifts her arms and wriggles
her hips and calls *yatehay!* to greet me.

> One hot summer we drove my blue Pinto
> to Truth or Consequences, New Mexico,
> to listen to a washed-up country crooner
> rasp his top hits through tinny speakers.
> The radiator blew driving back. We sang
> *rolling me down the highway* behind a tow truck
> those 90 miles to home.
> The next night we crossed over
> to Juarez to shoot Davy Crocketts till dawn.

That oak is an odd standout—she keeps her leaves all year.
Autumn, she's a mad dance of neon tangerine apricot salmon.
First winter snap, her notched leaves fade
to russet and hang there like loss until spring.

> Jody gave me her heart-
> leafed philodendron when she moved to NYC.
> Its green vines climbed the walls
> of every home I've had these 30 years since.
> Her letters came a few times a year, handwriting
> curvy, each word lifting off the page with a kick.
> Divorce, drinking, recovery,
> third marriage. I wanted to see her.

It's April again. Lime green leafbuds
push the ruddy weathered leaves to the street.

       I tell Jody I've searched for her online
       as we stroll past the oak to the park.
       When I found her obituary, I was left wanting
       to know how she died. I ask her
       to tell me, but she just says
       she loves the yellow balsamroot
       blooming everywhere we walk.

We Return to Our Regularly Scheduled Programing

after the first line of "Snow Man" by Wallace Stevens

You must have a stomach for chopped salad
to survive the evening news. The announcer
wedges his voice into your kitchen where you

dice cucumbers and plum tomatoes
for the Greek dinner you'll serve to guests.
There would be no television on if

you had your way. So, captive, you learn
the envoy carrying humanitarian relief in a convoy
of trucks was bombed into crumbs,

twenty peacekeepers killed, you don't catch
by whom. *That could have been me*, your daughter
yells at the TV, her good intentions

rising. *Please set the table,* you reply, breaking
feta into the bowl you toss by hand. Jon Snow
is driving a luxury car, the camera pans

his rugged face close-up to pique the appetites
of women and men across America who've
come home from work. The doorbell rings.

You turn off the tube and catch the scent
of lemon and oregano fortifying your hands.

City Council Meeting #3

The 12-acre lot is the first
to raise a hand. It speaks
of quail rookery and wind. No
translator is provided.
Teachers take turns,
tell of clogged roads
that cull kids. *Razing
is the future*, a young
councilman says. *Bull
dozers will lift the aspen
grove by the roots.*

Tragicomedy often begins
with a balding man
who can't see the forest
or the trees.

One neighbor reports the ground
is evacuating the perimeter.
The old pine trees
are warmed by their
new orange scarves. Or
did she say *warned*?
Neighbors find the orange
ribbons near their homes.
They would save them
all, if they could.
The trees
don't know what's coming.

Frida Kahlo Paints the Antarctic Forest

"A rainforest that flourished in Antarctica 90 million years ago is locked under the ice"
~ Discover Magazine, *1 April 2020*

My head spins since I learned of the frozen rain forest.
I want to paint that *selva, pero* what pigments
to make trees locked in ice nearly forever?
The color of a tree's bark tells the story of its spine.
I'll work with the browns I used in *Wounded Deer,*
pero I'll add a wash of blue for ice that seeped
into each grain, the way steam from a *caldo* can be tasted
on my lover's face after we've dined. It gets inside.
I am hungry for these trees. I can see
ochre and russet and sienna bleeding
in the bark held motionless like a woman
suspended in bed with a body cast, her spine
straightened like a bent pole. My friend
fears invisible germs killing people *por todo el mundo,*
like infinitesimal arrows pierce
and kill a deer. I fear what we can see—a streetlamp
stabs a city bus and the woman inside who a moment
before was gazing at small patches of sky.
Our futures impaled before
we can reach them, pasts
frozen before we can see them.
Mainly, I wonder what happened
to the leaves, if they were able to hold on
to their greens, if emeralds and parakeets
diminished to crocodiles and olives. *Ay,* thinking *sobre colores*
makes my hands itch for my brushes and paints.
My perspective will be standing above the treetops
looking down through clear frozen water, a few
ripples of mud. *Posiblemente* I will paint
parrots in the branches. Our sorrows
are the same colors as our pains.
I was once a tree frozen in ice

From Mrs. Mallard's Diary

for the protagonist of "The Story of an Hour" by Kate Chopin,
the day before she died of a "broken heart"

The meager heat
of our upstairs room
chills my bones.
I see treetops
out my window.
I would like
to perch there
and preen.
I'm a baffled sparrow
glimpsing her reflection
in the glaze.

Fast trains were built for men,
women
for the slow
burn of days.

His repeated pleasantries
are the pearls I wear
around my neck.
They chafe when I chirp.

I am the house pet.
I like to coo.
It makes me grow
wings. This folly helps
pass time. I fold my wants
next to the white hankies
I store in this box.

Open Letter to Sun, After a Long Winter

O Sunshine, bolt to us from your roost. Heat this city
   block with its corralled gardens and porches, even
      the blue house with the canary-yellow trim on the corner
         and the house banked by cedars across the street.

Rush past all those celestial orbs
   to this street and my house where I've lived
      with one person for months and no visitors.
         Shine your searching spotlight on our alone.

Drive out afternoon darkness that sullied our porches
   with early night, romp on my garden bed, touch your fiery hands
      to the bluegrass's reedy throats and these dull sidewalks
         where dramas occasionally unfold that need

to be examined in all kinds of light.
   Find where I hide from my daughter, my friends, behind
      books, on the inside of these windows and walls.
         Reach for me in these shadows, where I wait.

Blazing a Trail

I find all kinds of things on the sidewalk—
an empty wallet, wadded receipt, yesterday's silver
-rimmed beer can, a man with a handkerchief
wound around his bloodied head.
Neighbors called, afraid
he would die there.

I'm pretty sure the injured man
wanted a road map and lantern,
maybe a message in Morse code
tapping its dits and dahs in his ear
like a drum, or chug of smoke signals
some gods might billow above the ER
to mark his trail's end.

These are the steps
death takes: the organs fight
for blood, especially the brain. It will
suck the blood up from the feet
with unrelenting thirst. This in turn
turns the feet blue. Blue the color of absence,
blue that creeps up the legs slowly,
visibly, like a bar graph might demonstrate
the progress of loss.

Sun to Shade

The last month my mother was alive,
   she couldn't speak, she sat in the wheelchair
      and chomped her mouth like an old miner.
         Melanoma drilled shafts in her brain.
            While she rested, my dad swept

the kitchen tiles where once a year
   her sisters lifted their spatulas and sang
      harmony like the Lennon sisters.
         Then silence sat on the reupholstered couch,
            which was vacuumed and set out on the curb

in the sunlight. Sunlight replaced
   the chatter and the dull thud of the front door
      when it opened and shut. Dad lived alone there
         in the flatlands of summer, with a healthy
            freezer full of casseroles, and full boxes

he moves today to an apartment with all of its
   windows sealed shut. His new neighbors
      are strange as the swans on the desert
         golf course. He sits alone in the patio gazebo
            listening to new voices in the distance.

Driftwood

My dad's final days unfurl
slowly, like an arthritic hand.
I bend over him, study his face
like a seashell. I watch the small nook
in his neck tick each heartbeat. He waves
me away.
           When he leaves, what will happen
to my hands? I suppose they'll become seagulls
perched on a log on the Oregon coast
where he searched for seashells
with his siblings when all six had aged
to white hair, white as the silver dollars
they collected in plastic bags. I'm afraid
my wings won't know how
to lift off from the driftwood
and take air. Hunger,
                    like a father,
will push them to scavenge
a nibble of seaweed. They
won't go far from where they perched.
Tangerine clouds will whisper
the darkness is coming to fold your wings.
While they sleep, waves will
lap softly as a fringe of small bubbles
takes the beach one handful
of sand at a time.

Blowing Through

Just this morning, I touched his silver hair
and balmed the surgical wound on his scalp.
While he napped, the scent of creosote traveled
across the courtyard through the open balcony door
where I packed crystal bells
and the carved mahogany cranes
with impossibly slender necks.
I stood on the balcony and closed my eyes
to the bright January sun. At night, the sun

slips over the black mountains to the west where stars
outnumber lives. Black highways taper
toward that craggy horizon, beyond city limits
where developments pock the desert's crusty hide.
This is where families bring their loved ones
to die. They don't know they're going
to die. The backyards have astro-turf lawns.
No one goes outside. I seal

more boxes and tidy his apartment,
sit in his recliner to sort months of piled mail.
Before I leave, he asks me to sing that song again,
he can't remember the name, I should
know it, so I sing the one I want to hear
until the car pulls up to collect me
and my father disappears in the desert.

Driving through Wheat Fields to Waitsburg

You, road, I enter upon and look around, I believe you are not all that is
here, I believe that much unseen is also here.
~ Walt Whitman "Song of the Open Road"

It is October. No rain will fall from this
blue platter sky. Gold wheat crops
checker the landscape. A few harvested fields
turn their blank faces towards me.
Their mouths are full of dirt clods
that won't let them talk.

The farther south I drive, the steeper
the hills. They rise gradually,
like grief, until I'm driving in a canyon
with no horizon, buffalo grass
lined up like soldiers on both sides.
I'm heading for Waitsburg
where I've never been. I don't know
the way and I'm out of cell range. No matter
how far I drive, he won't be there to greet me.
Sometimes a friend must die before you
realize he was a prophet.

I pull into the dirt lot below the cemetery.
The others have gathered on the hill,
dark coats like a congregation of crows
looking down at an empty gum wrapper.
I join the family graveside. I know
only my friend's wife. We link arms
until I stand and read Whitman
to my friend who has become
the breeze that carries the psalm
I sing into the open hand of sky.

Into Each Day Some Blueberry Must Fall

Lift your intentions when your hands sift through dirt—
it's the only way to finger the insides of rocks.

Don't put all your sphagnum moss in one bucket. Spread
the load like hearts separate blood into chambers.

Impulses carry us down garden paths where indifferent
pebbles will never spill the secrets that fell from our mouths.

How many gardeners does it take to screw in one blueberry bush?
How many buckets of moss does it take to feed earth?

The soles of our shoes should be ashamed of their roots, a shame
we let go of when we thrust our hands into dirt.

House Call

Ligyrophobia stomps into my living room
        wearing a purple caftan and headdress, his
                auburn hair spiked out on all sides. Every

movement he makes sounds an alarm, like the boom
        when he sits on the couch. *I'm thirsty!* he shouts, so I
                brew a pot of chamomile tea to help him stay

calm. I don't know what prompted this house call. When he's
        not here, he visits women the age I was when we met—
                in their 20s, living behind locked doors

and windows, hearts pounding with each racing motor
        outside, each pump on the gas a carnivore's roar.
                What I want to say is my heart

is a growling lioness when he comes. She wants
        to tear his heart into small bits and eat them.
                Be afraid, her eyes say to him. *You have grown*

fat, I want to devour you. It's danger
        that weaves like a ghost outside the window.
                One thin sheet of glass is all

that kept him at bay. You know who I mean, dead
        for years and still the fear that revs up when I hear
                a loud engine. Ligyro slurps the blond tea

from my grandmother's china cup lined with silver
        and pink roses. When he leaves, I see the hairline crack
                where he pressed his thumb too hard.

Three Spells

Once, I sprinkled a ring of salt
on the carpet of my room and stepped inside,
lit a blue candle, blessed each part
of my body with my fingers dipped in water and wine.
My body lived closer to bruises than tan lines.
I needed to be kissed
by my own hand.

The second time, I sprinkled salt
around my small house where the bricks
touch the ground, laying it thick
around windows and doors. I won't tell
the next step, but I can say it worked
against the intruder I meant to keep out.

The last time, I gathered Russian thistle
from the mountains hours from my house,
their purple heads belying barbed stems.
I rammed three black candles in the Bermuda grass
in the yard beneath the reach of a mulberry tree.
I chanted for the pain he gave others
to come back to him threefold.

A year later, he was shot
three times in the chest, and the man
who shot him was shot through his living room window
while he sat on his couch, and that man's assassin
was found dead under a freeway bridge two states away.
Spells were made by women with no other way
to tip the odds in their favor.

Rack of Ribs

My daughter tells me her dreams.
Last night, she was holding a bronze shovel
as she stood in front of her ex-boyfriend,
the one who said things to her
she wants to keep buried. She tried
to say something. Nothing came out.
He's the boy who scarred everyone he touched.
I dream about him too. I dream I'm
tying him up on the cement pad in the yard
where I notch his skin with pinpricks all over, place
one drop of handmade flammable oil
into each tiny pit. I torch him
with a disposable Bic I picked up on my way
past the convenience store on the corner.
I was raised to waste not, so not to waste
a good fire, we'll roast a calf over the flames, or
part of one—the ribs, so when the meat is cooked
all through like a slow-roasted trauma, we can tear
flesh off the bones and feast and feed what's left
to all the lost dogs in the neighborhood and the crows
that show up when they catch that first whiff
of meat. After we feast, we can
bury what's left under the maple trees
in the yard with my daughter's shiny shovel.

Harmony Comes to My Daughter's Apartment

My daughter climbs the stepstool to string
a web of pothos vines on the wall
that gets the most light. I see
the tattooed vines she doesn't want me to see
twining her upper arms and legs.
Harmony walks in and plops on the couch, dumps
her duffle on the floor and starts talking.
My daughter's just finished
a batch of bean soup.
                    Harmony sits across
from the vined wall, but she doesn't notice.
Her head is planted in her phone.
I step into the kitchen for some soup.
My daughter's learning to bake. Yesterday
she stirred up cupcakes from scratch, whipped
strawberries into pink icing with a pinch
of agave.
            I can't tell if Harmony
will move in or stay just the night.
Now they're taking about women's oppression:
Women have always been raped.
We've read the Greek myths since 7th grade.
Even female animals are forced
to incubate young.
                    As I slip out,
I hear *we are all walking wombs,*
though she might have said *wounds.*
They'll stay up talking
half the night, will share their plans
for the next inked lines that will spread
up their legs and arms like walls
protected by vines.

Elisa Learns to Box

for the protagonist of John Steinbeck's "The Chrysanthemums"

We've been working on my stance.
Lane's dragged a line in the dirt with his boot.
My feet must straddle the line, diagonal,
wider than my shoulders, elbows down,
and my hands must be up, but not my
everyday hands. My hands must be fists,
which takes getting used to, so I think of them
as flower bulbs for planting.

Lane wraps my garden
rags around my hands thick as gloves
I'm to keep in front of my head,
chin tucked. I practice
when no one is watching.

I wearied of the pity I sprinkled on
myself like a leaky water can in need
of repair. Now my blood
races each week I stride the trail
to the toolshed where Lane's bunked for summer.

Tomorrow we start on punches
and jabs. Lane tells me to breathe, but I
can't breathe when I think of
landing a blow. I can't feature myself boxing
outside of this shed. If I plant
my fist in a jaw, what will grow?

The Middle Hannah Speaks

*after Hannah Maynard's Self-portrait with multiple exposure
(circa 1893)*

I see my two other selves
on either side of me
from this framed perch
in the wall.
You, Miss Priss
to my right, you
grate my last nerve, pouring
tea like a servant. A small pot is
all a woman like you can handle.
Your heart's sealed off.
The bear rug does nothing
to toughen you.

And you, on my left,
face scrubbed of emotion, your gaze
breaks the fourth wall like a punch. You're
my kind of dame. Our kind can
put our own teenage child in a box
and let men bury her in the dirt
under the old oak with bent arms
while we bury ourselves in black
broadcloth.

With my camera, I create
life as I'd like it. Three of me
in one frame means there's less
weight for each of us to bear. We've
hung here too long. Let's bust
out of this frame, break
the good china, build
a mosaic life from the shards.
I christen you both my Calliope
with this stream from my cup.
Then I smash it to pieces.

Love Poem to Roasted Cashews

I love the curve of each body,
one end a slightly swollen bulb,
tan like god's own
modeling clay for making
a woman who wants
to arch her back and beckon
sunlight to caress the full
length of her neck.
When I bite down,
the cashew doesn't
fight me but gives in
to the grate and grind
of my teeth, again
like a woman who's been made
to feel safe and so
surrenders to her lover's
touch, becoming meal,
a mixture of meat and saliva
that's no trouble to swallow,
take into herself,
fulfilled.

Love Poem to My Garden Blueberries

I want to be a blueberry in my garden.
I want to feel tender touches that test me

and the firm tugs that cascade my ripe
into a hungry hand. I want blueberry

skin, wax-white then green then blushed
by sun turning me purple without shame.

I want green-fleshed muscle, dark
with thirst. I want a name inspired

by my spill from the red oracle of want.
I want to stain birds warbling their fill. I want

purple skin polished to silver memories
of fed. I want to be a blueberry near sisters

with hands that can touch them.
I want to be a small fruit of longing

because one large cluster of it
would be too much to bear.

Private Message to Sun from a Heliophilic Friend

I watch you enter full throttle down my street
like a sailor on shore leave. You're wearing
a shiny new civilian suit you bought for attention.
You'll get it. Please forgive me, though,
as the day chugs on I get distracted
by a pan of morning eggs, the hunt
for a book, what should I wear
with this shirt. Phone calls.
Emails. Going out to buy mirepoix
for an easy pot of soup.

Let's make a deal: I'll mind you
each time I'm up at daybreak.
I'll savor the soft colors your warm lungs
exhale on the horizon.
I'll also tend to your settings, will
witness the purple and red sheets you hang
backstage of the sky, colored like wine
you pressed from all those distant grapes.

Your job is to look after yourself
in the long arc in between
while I fill my emptied glass with amber
tea, teach poems and persuasion
online, escort my old dog
outside and back in.

Listen, already the birds
have hushed in the trees. See the lights
springing on in windows down the block?
That's my neighbors.
Every nightfall we turn on
framed portraits of your light.

Acknowledgements

Grateful appreciation is given to the editors of the following journals and anthologies in whose pages these poems or their earlier versions first appeared.

All We Can Hold (Sage Hill Press): "From the Well"
American Poetry Journal: "To Protect Your Brother's Young Sons" and
       "Truth is"
Border Voices Anthology (Vergin Press): "Nothing We Did Before"
5 AM: "The Whiskers on His Face"
California Quarterly: "Night's Coming"
Cathexis Northwest Press: "Dream #3: Spilled Milk" and "Dream #11:
       Peeping Tom"
Cirque: "The Shape of My Hand"
Citron Review: "Tarot Reading: The Hanged Man (inverted)"
Concho River Review: "Oology"
Comstock Review: "Daily Bread"
Essential Love: Poems About Mothers & Fathers, Daughters & Sons
       (Poetworks of Grayson Books): "Nestling"
Eclectica: "Chemistry" and "We Watched for Falling Stars"
Minerva Rising: "Harvest" and "Under the Beds"
Night Music Journal: "Driving through Wheat Fields to Waitsburg"
The Oval: "He Carried My Voice"
Raw Art Review: "Punch Line," "I Wish This Tree Were My Friend Jody,"
       and "Frida Kahlo Paints the Antarctic Forest"
RHINO: "Trees, Paper, Time, Hands"
Rio Grande Review: "Tarot Reading: Passion (Inverted)" and "I Let Go My
       Grip"
Rock & Sling: "Sun to Shade"
The Shore: "I come to know thirst," and "Steps To Protect Your Young Child"
Sin Fronteras / Writers without Borders: "It Never Came Back"
Slipstream: "Aubade, with Open Hand"
Streetlight Magazine: "The Day His Dad Died" and "Vault"
Sycamore Review: "Slaughterhouse"
Times of Sorrow, Times of Grace: Writing by Women of the Great Plains
       (Backwaters Press): "The Whiskers on His Face"
Wild Roof: "Motion of Rocks"
Women. Period. (Spinsters Ink): "Tracking Orbs"

"I Wish This Tree Were My Friend Jody" was the First Runner-Up and "Frida Kahlo Paints the Antarctic Rain Forest" was a Runner-Up in *Raw Art Review's* William Carlos Williams Prize for Poetry.

Special and heartfelt thanks to Moonstone Press for publishing the first part of this book as a chapbook, *Predictable as Fire* (2021).

Connie Wasem Scott was born in Greeley, Colorado to a family of four who camped and skied in the Rockies. Her brother Chuck was her constant companion when they were children and her close friend into adulthood until his complicated and untimely death. Their parents were raised in North Dakota, and the four spent many summers there. When she was 12, her family moved to El Paso, TX, and the moved prompted her to start writing poems. In college, she took a contemporary American poetry class, which was her bona fide initiation to the artform. Connie came to love El Paso and its arid landscape, endless sky, and blended cultures. She earned a BA in Literature and an MA in Professional Writing and Rhetoric from UT El Paso, where she subsequently joined the faculty and taught a variety of English courses as a full-time lecturer for 9 years. In time, she sought a tenured position to give her young daughter stability, which led her in 2001 to Spokane, WA, and she's been teaching a variety of writing and literature courses at Spokane Falls Community College ever since. She spends as much time as she can outdoors—camping, hiking, kayaking and canoeing with her Aussie-American husband Alexander. She also thrives on the escapades, dramas, and tender moments she shares with her daughter Makenna. Connie loves forested mountains and arid deserts, tartar sauce with fries and green chile cheese enchiladas, thick socks in winter boots and colorful toenails in flip flops.

www.ingramcontent.com/pod-product-compliance
Lightning Source LLC
Chambersburg PA
CBHW021154090426
42740CB00008B/1084